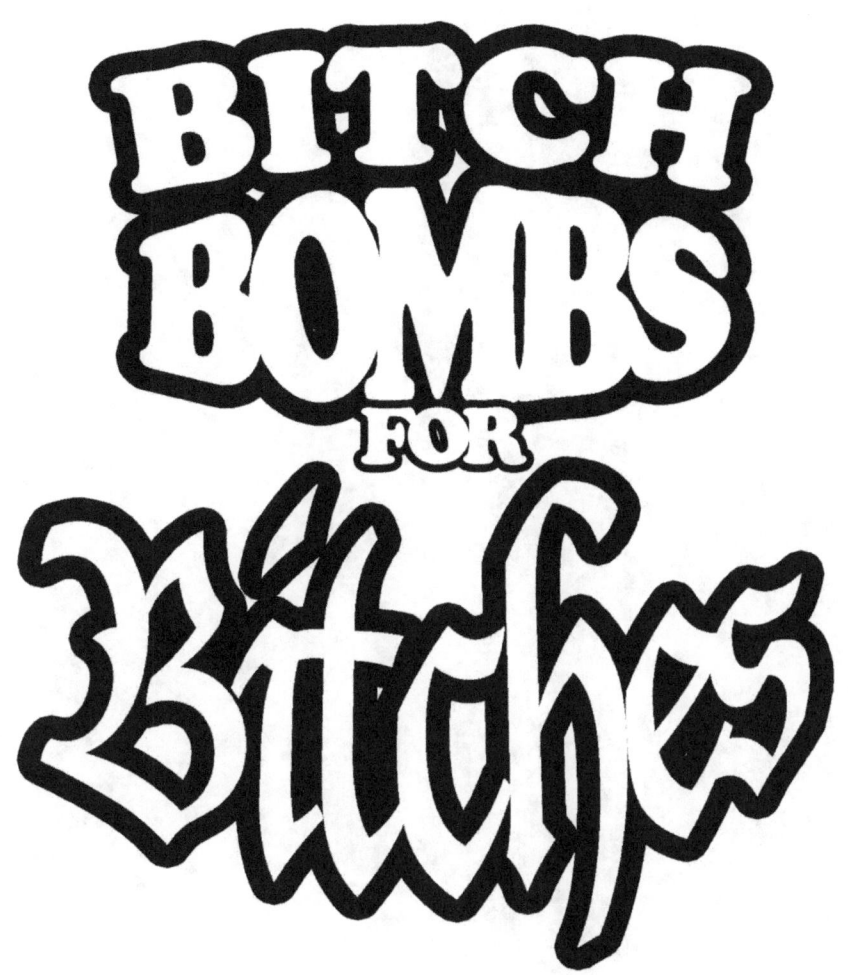

SWEAR WORD COLORING BOOK

Kate Blume
blumesberry art

Page Addie Press

ISBN:978-0-6480768-0-3 paperback.
BIC Subject category: 1. Arts & Photography. 2. Drawing-coloring books for grown-ups
3. Craft, hobbies 4. Self-help-art therapy & relaxation 5. Self-help-anger management

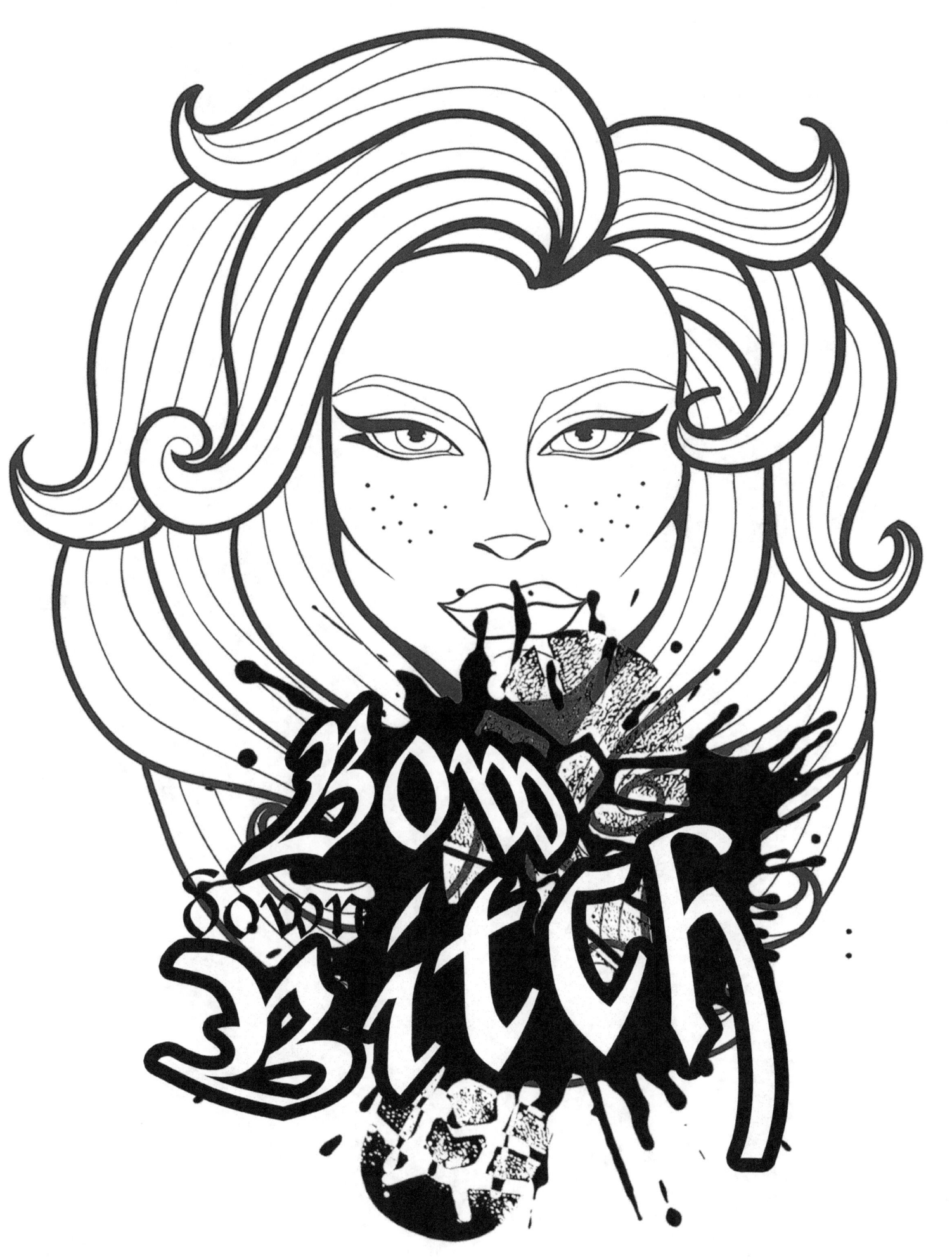

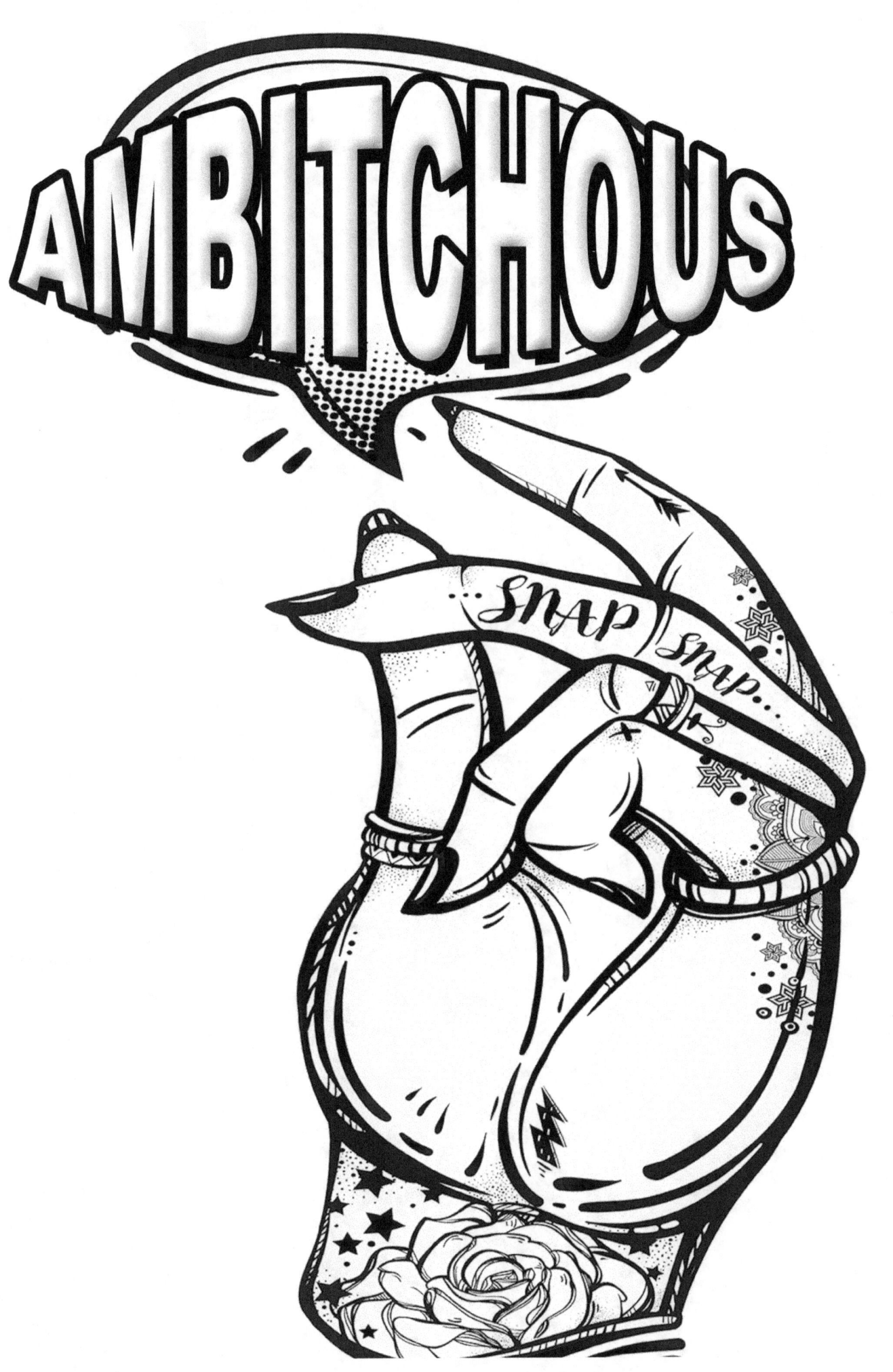

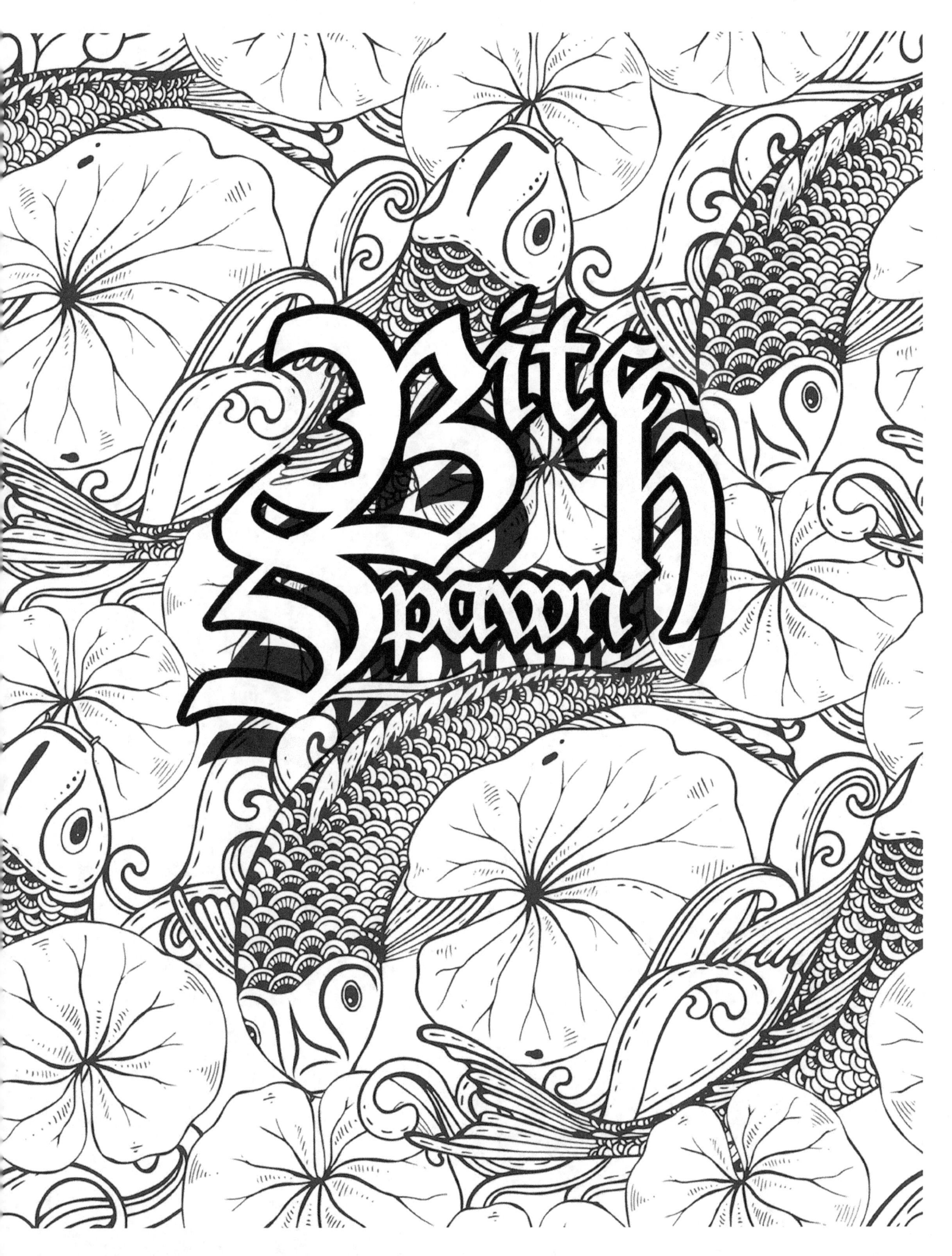

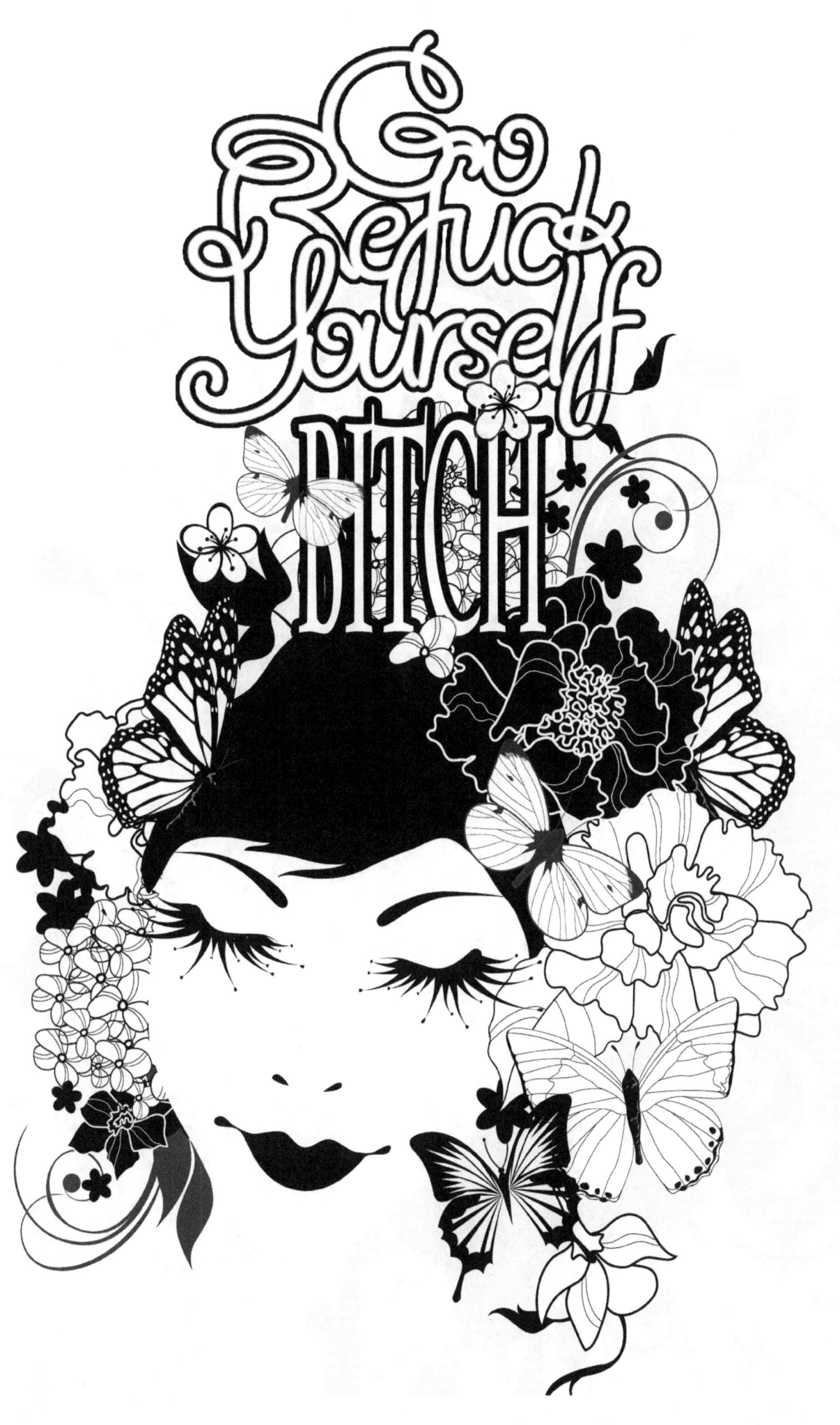

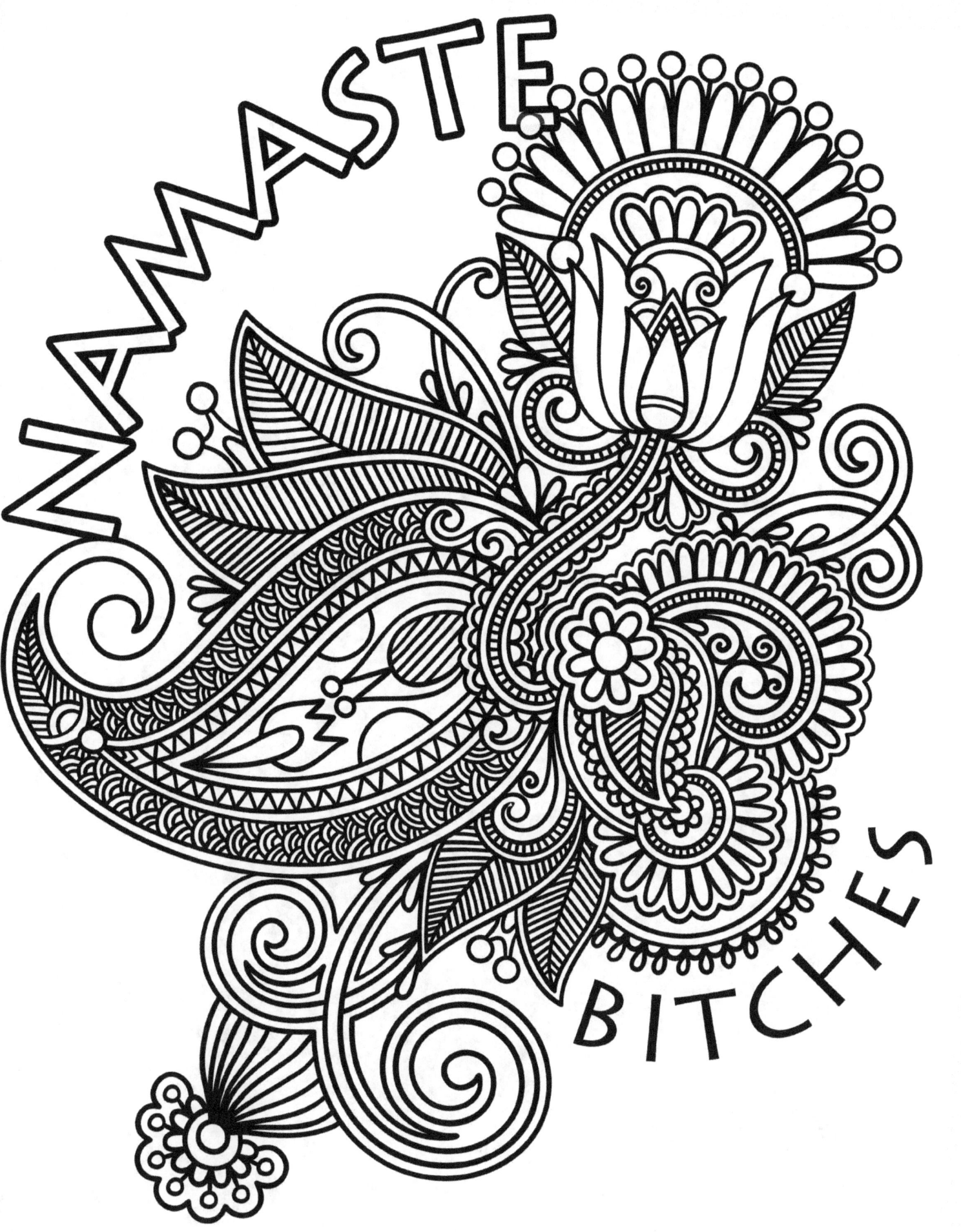

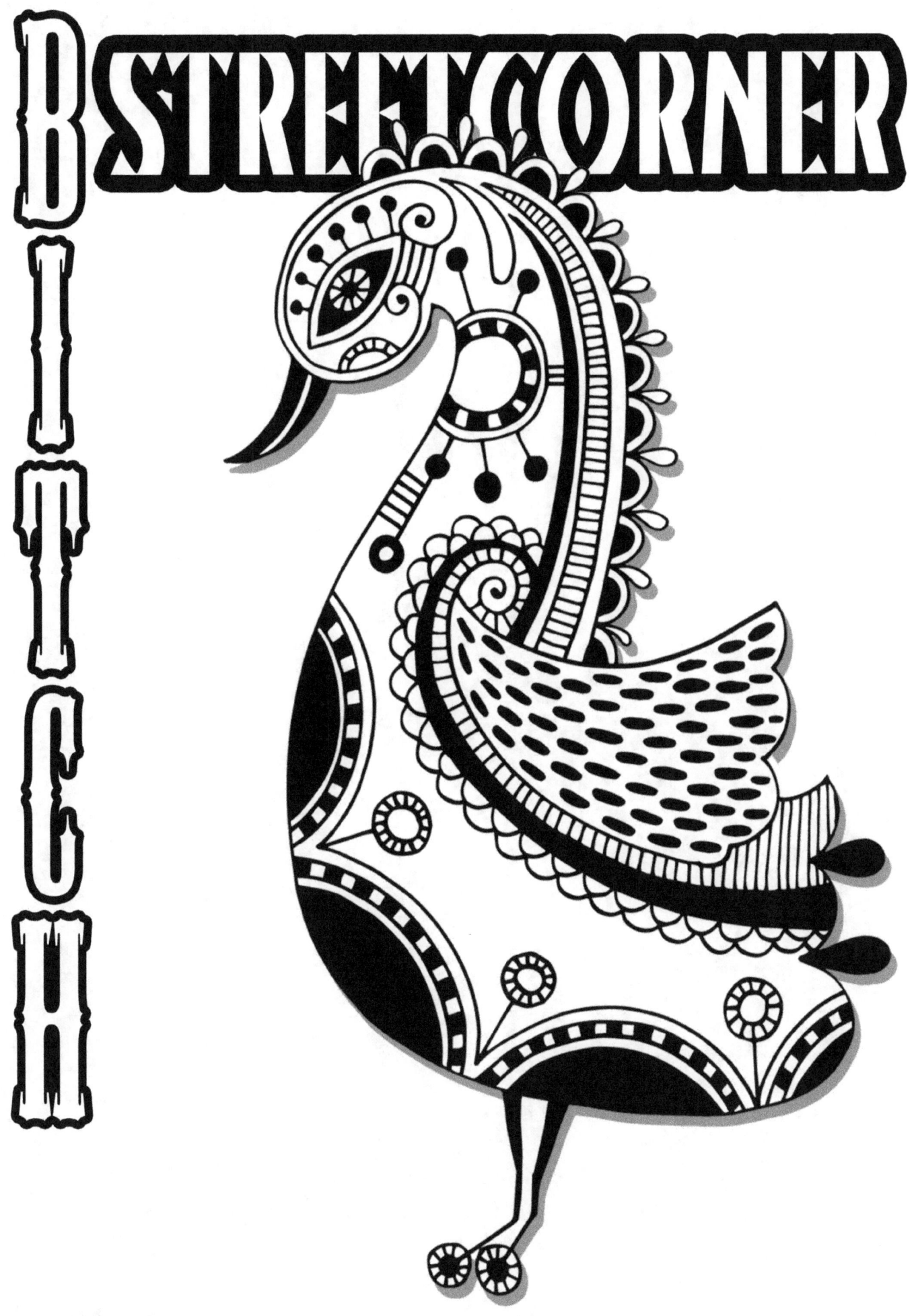

BITCH

STREETCORNER

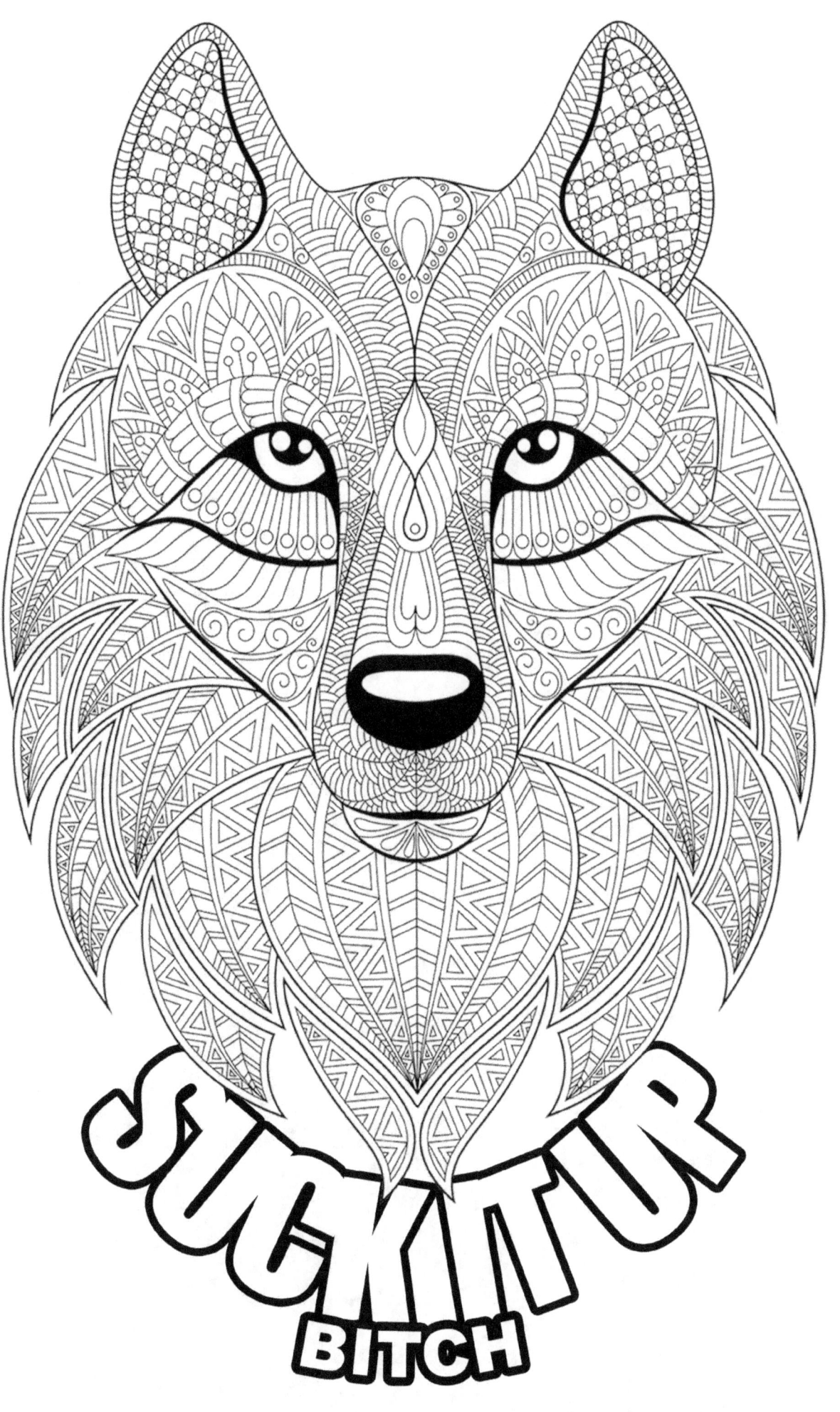

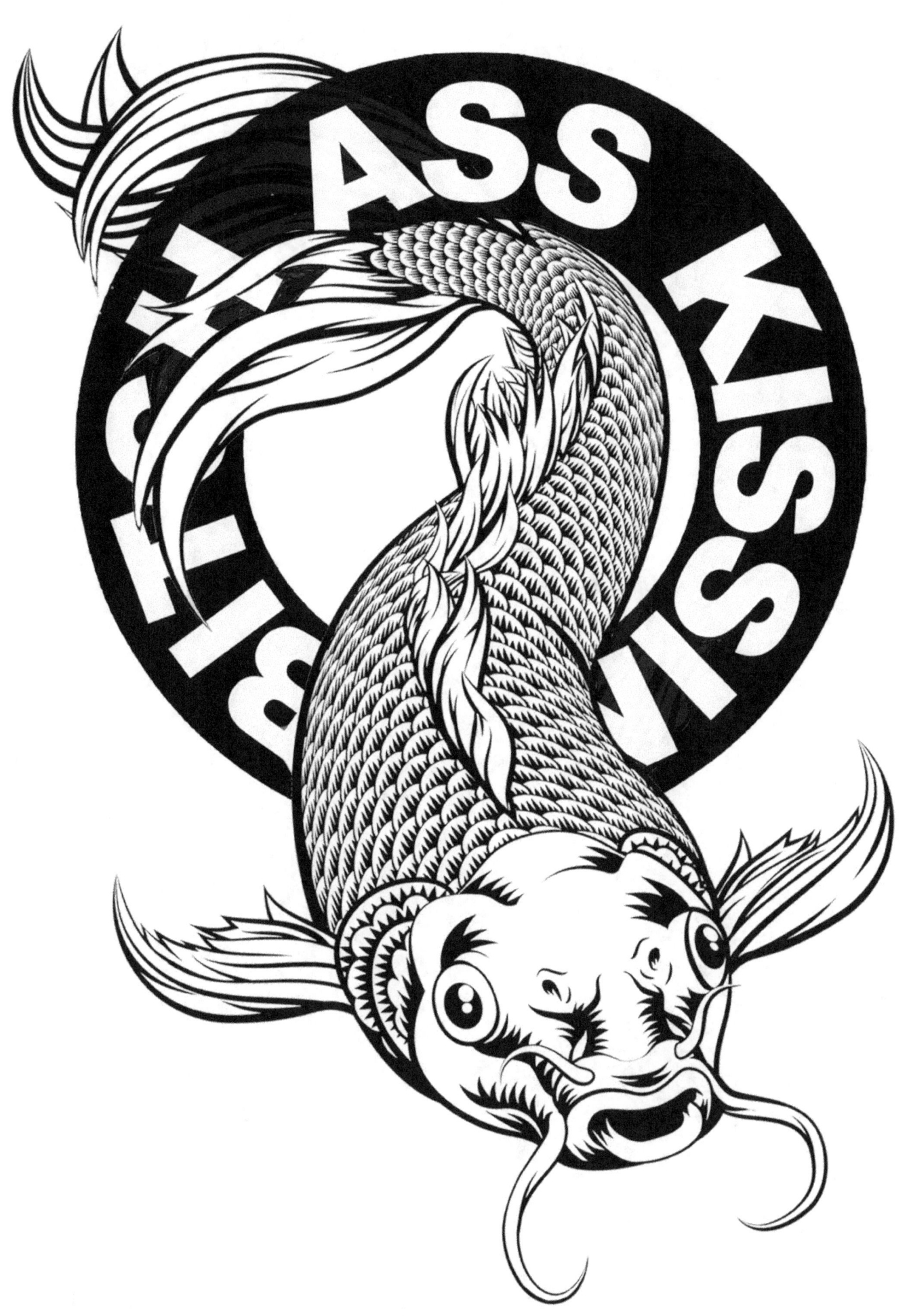

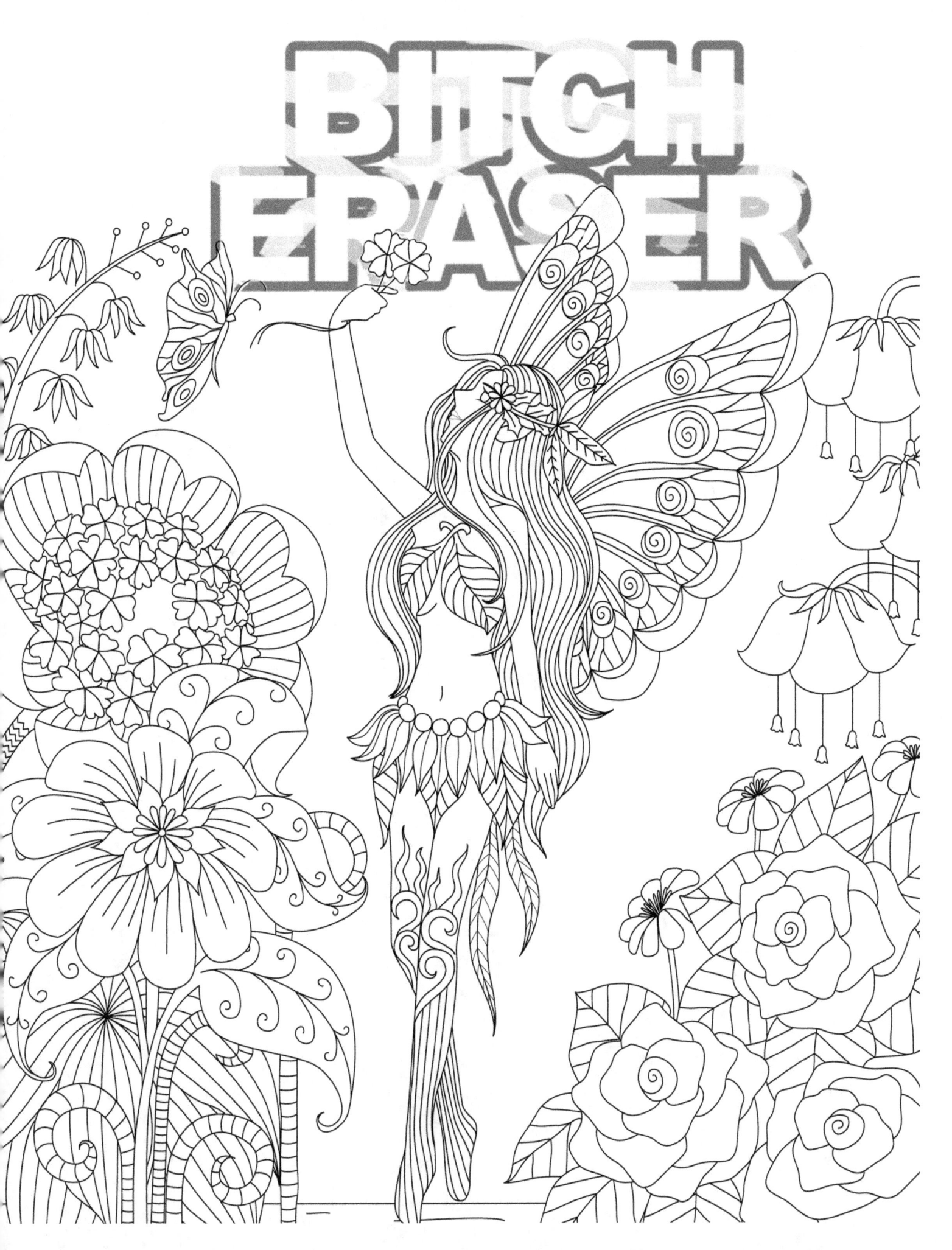

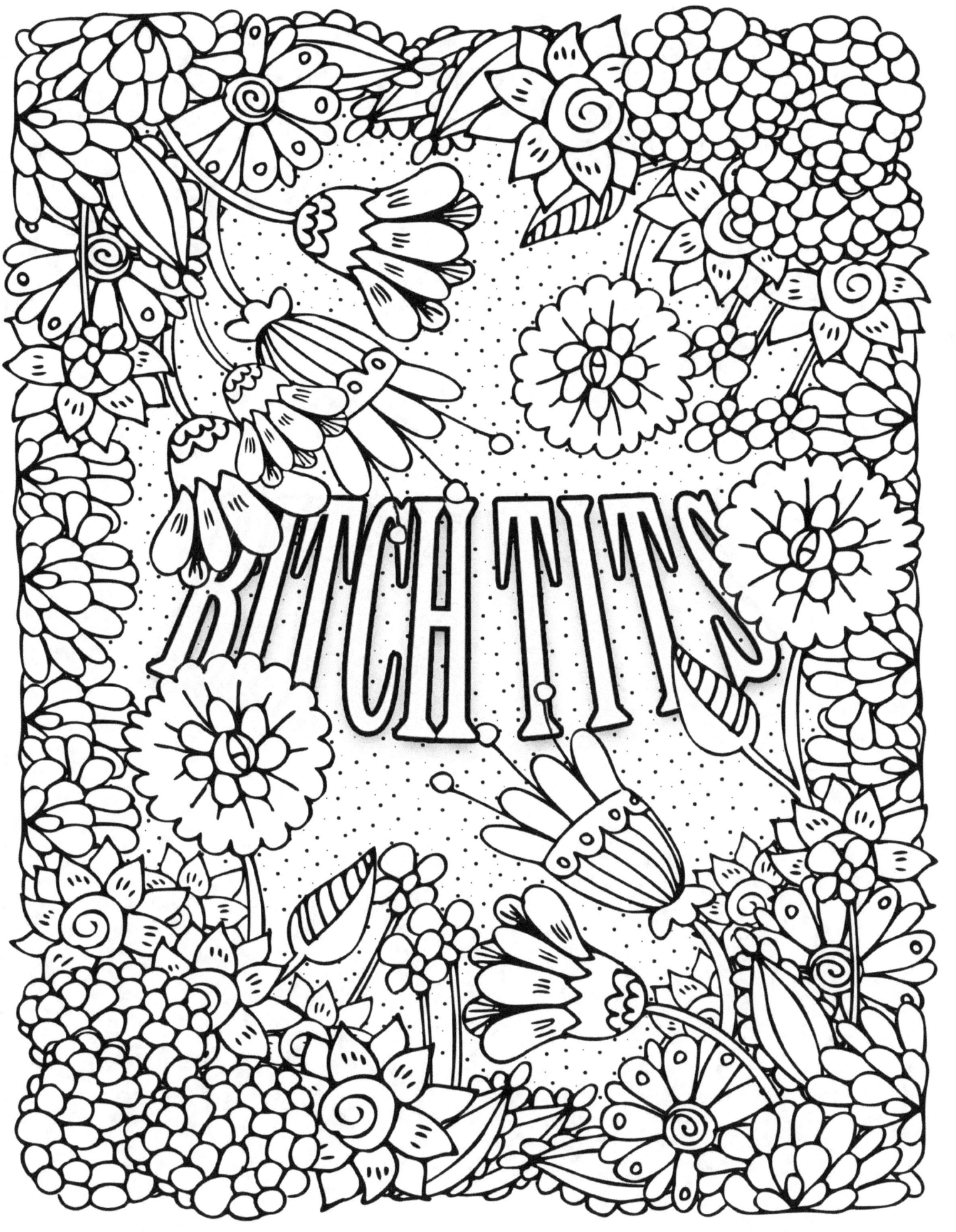

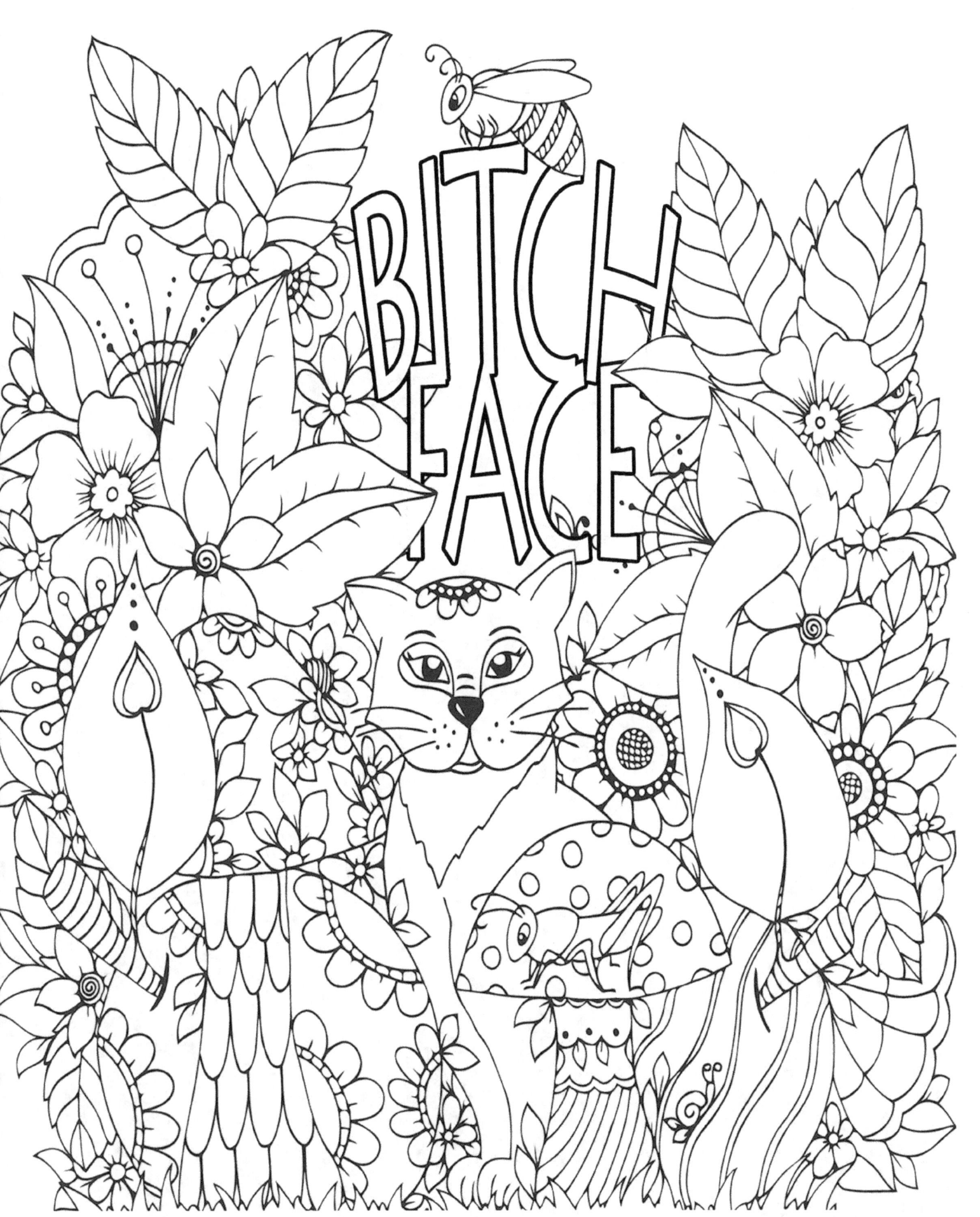

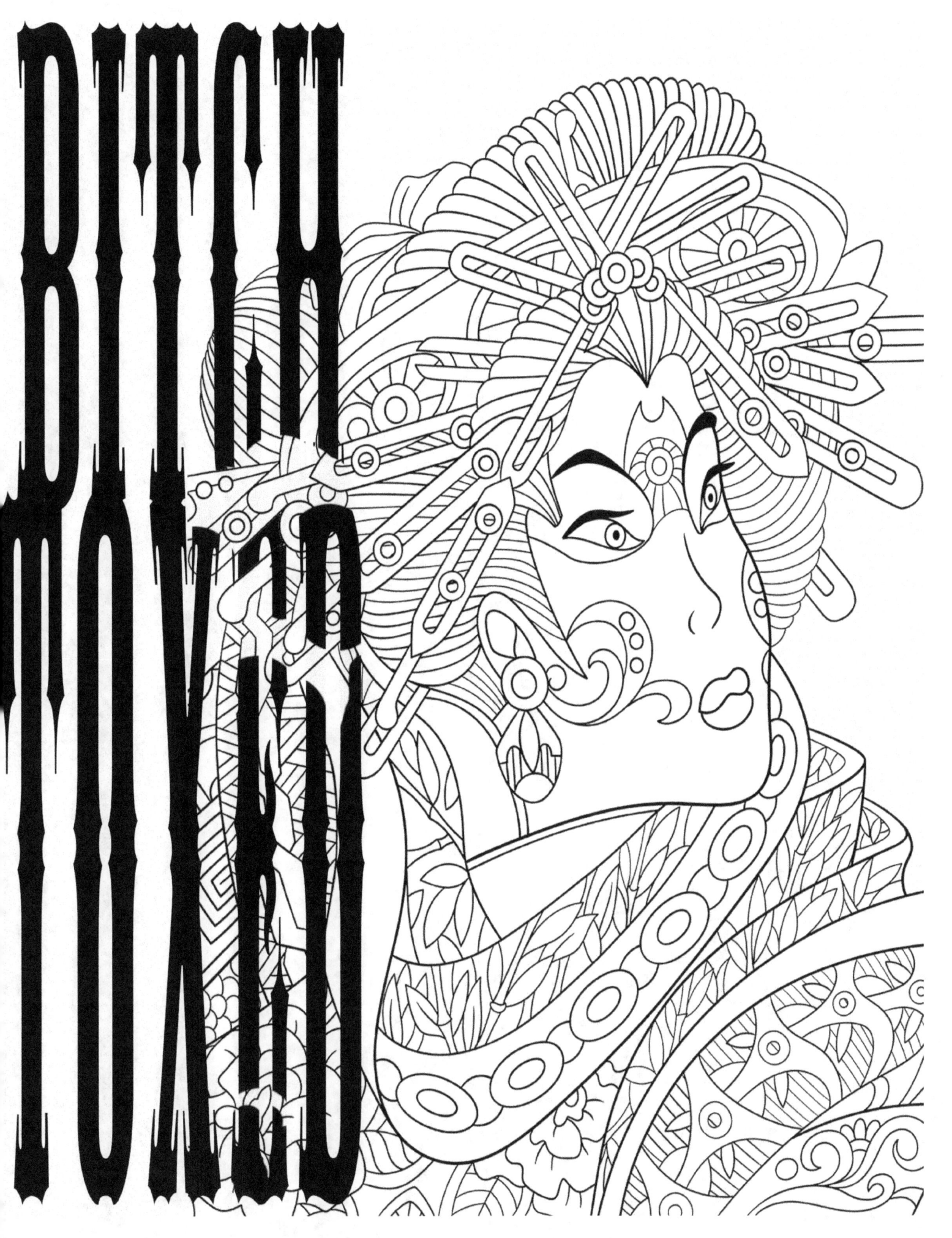

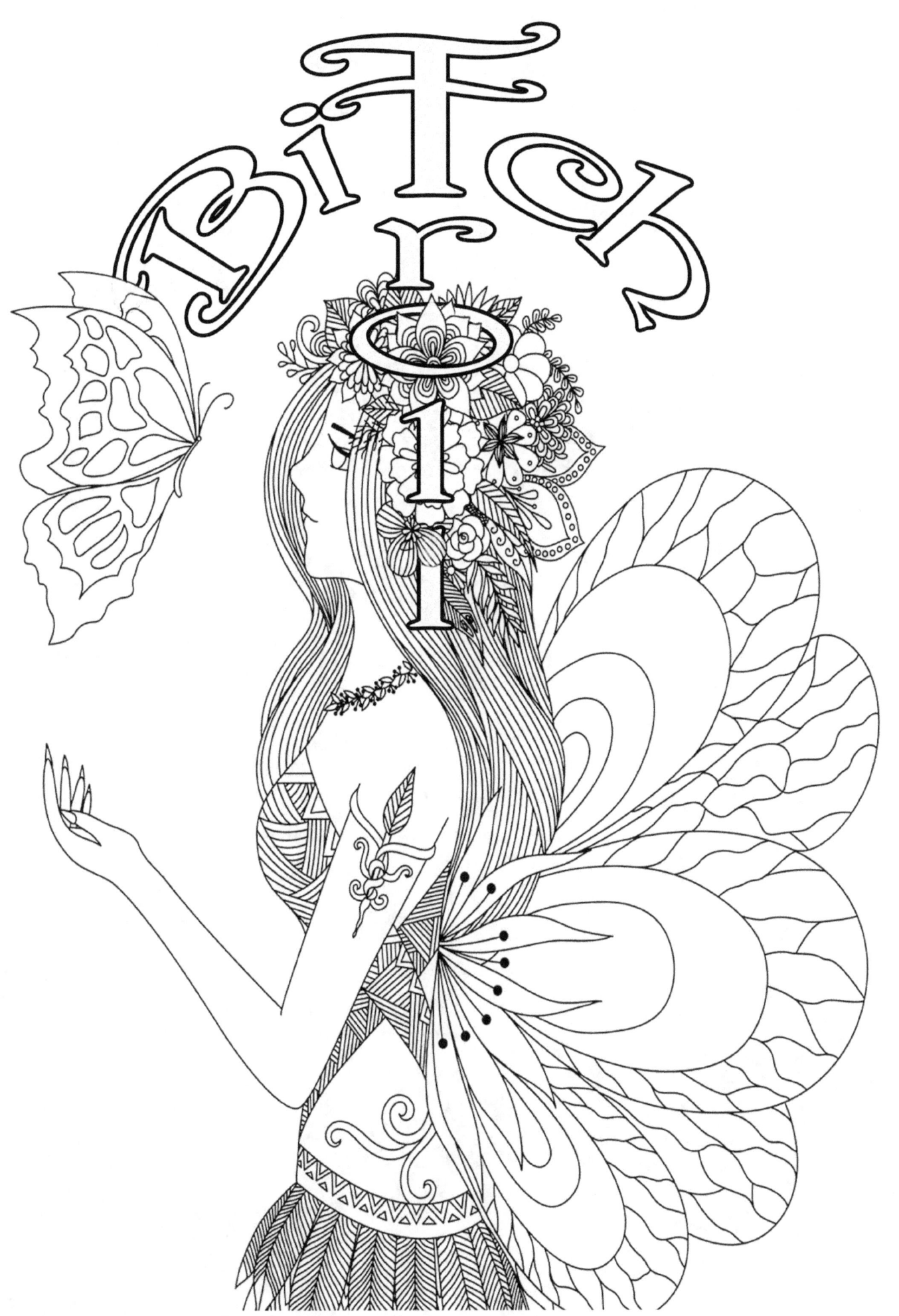

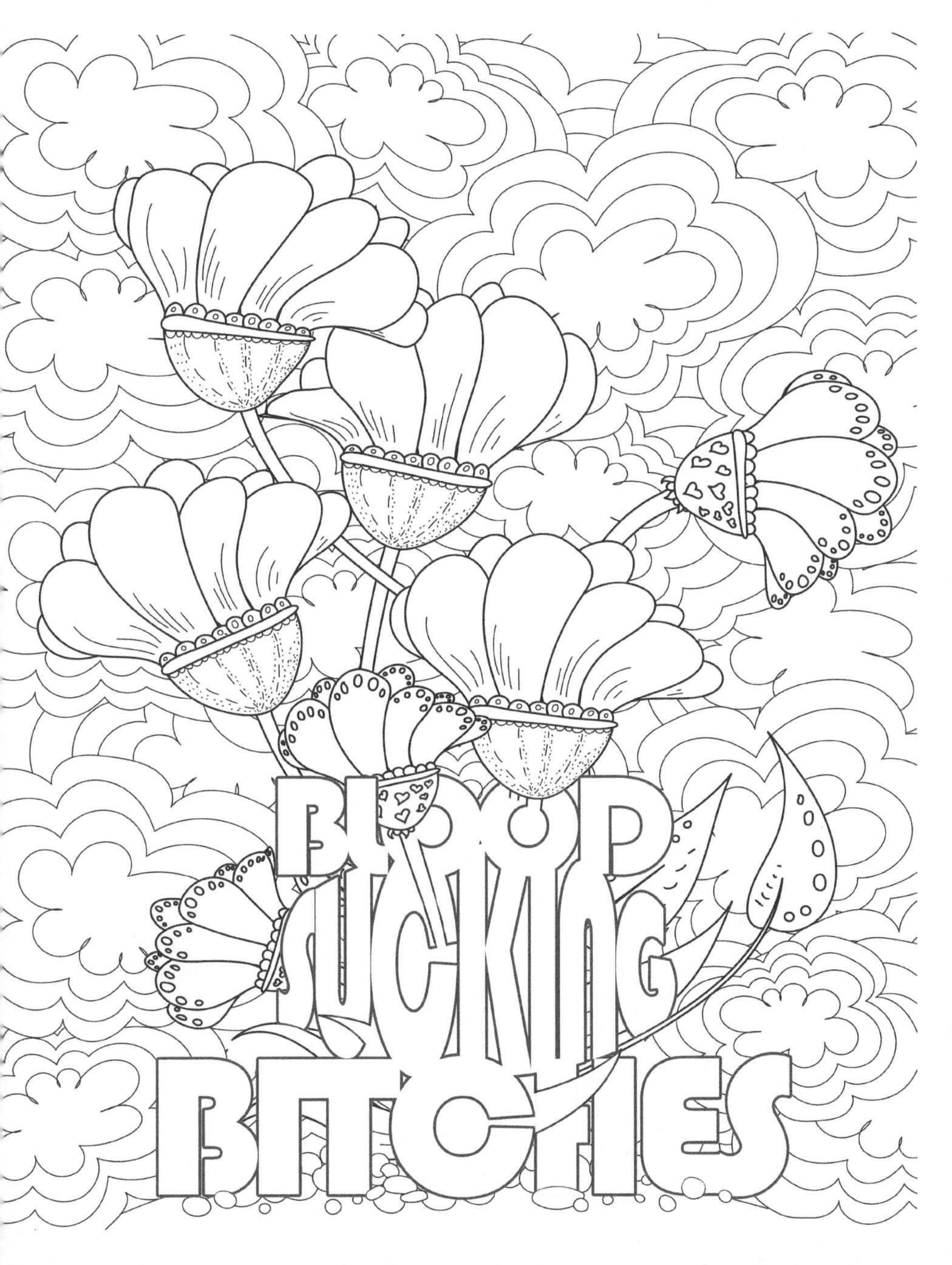

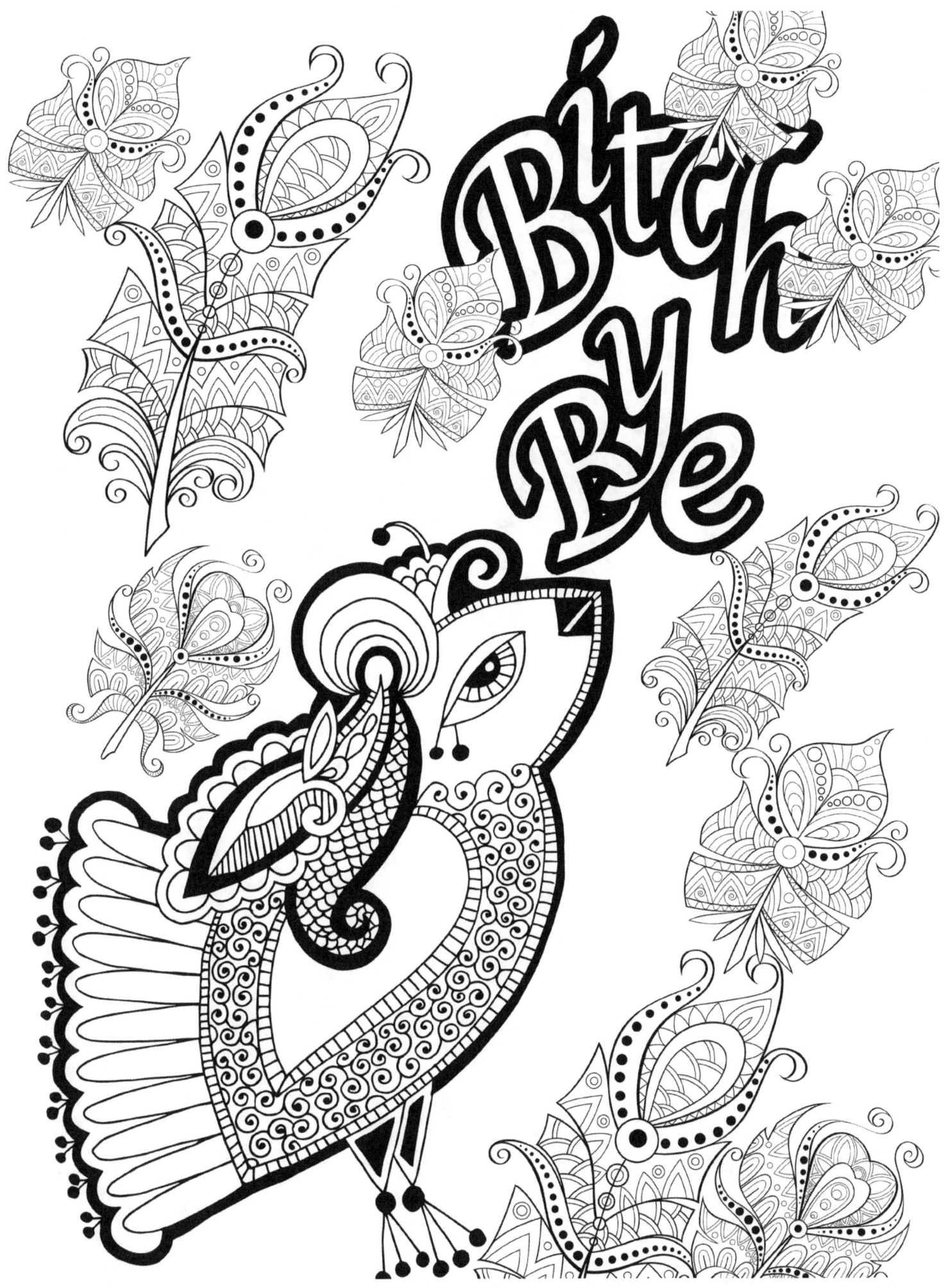

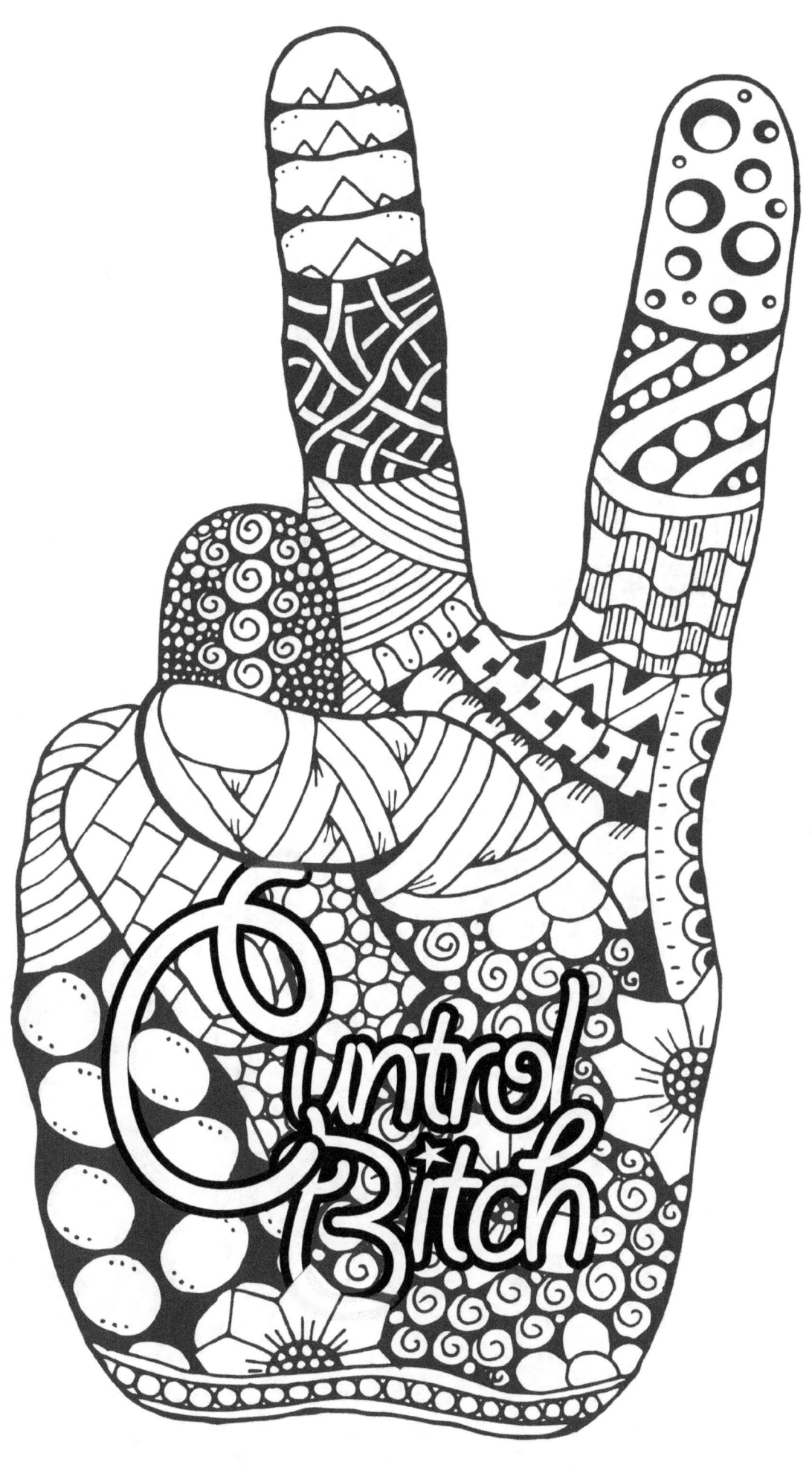

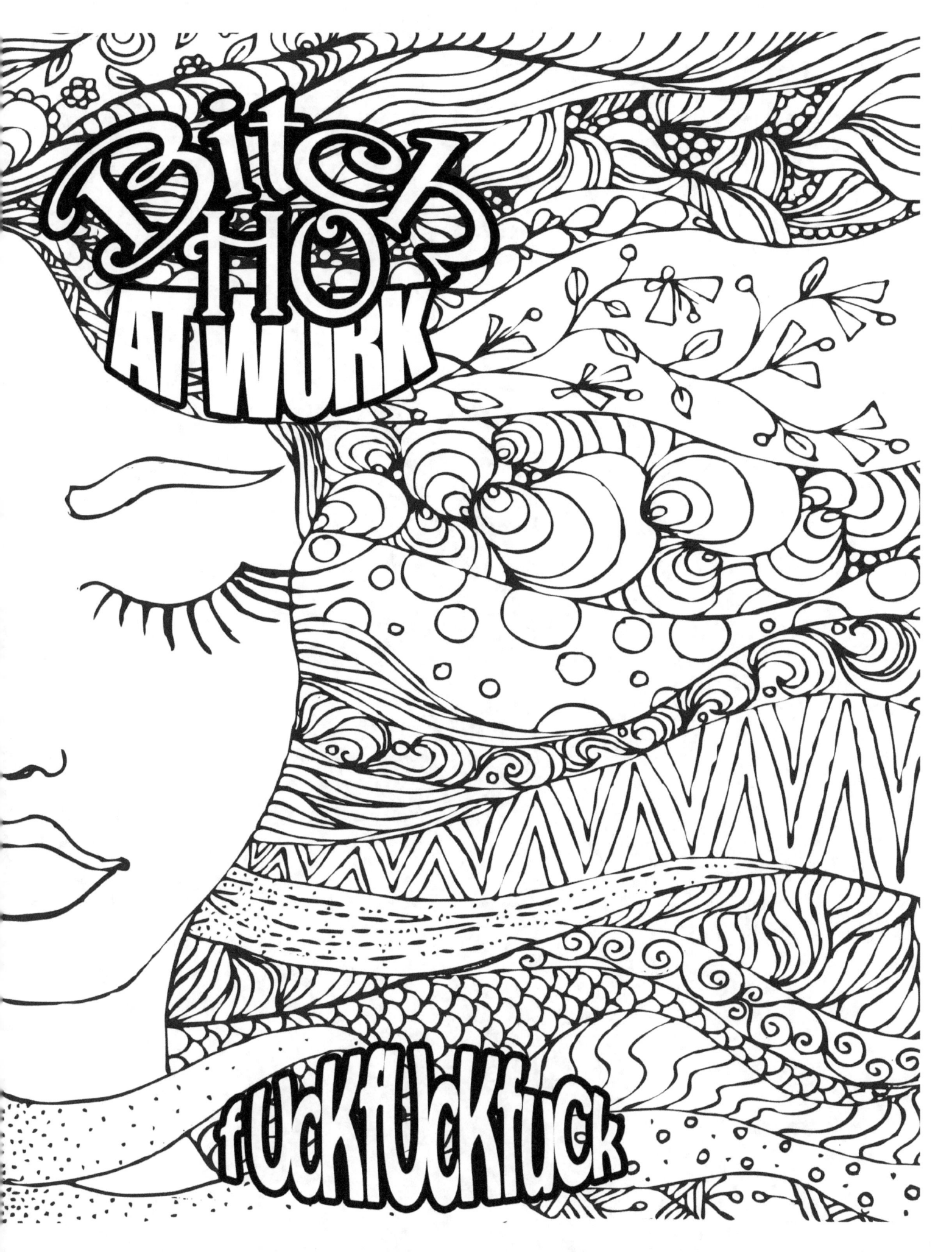

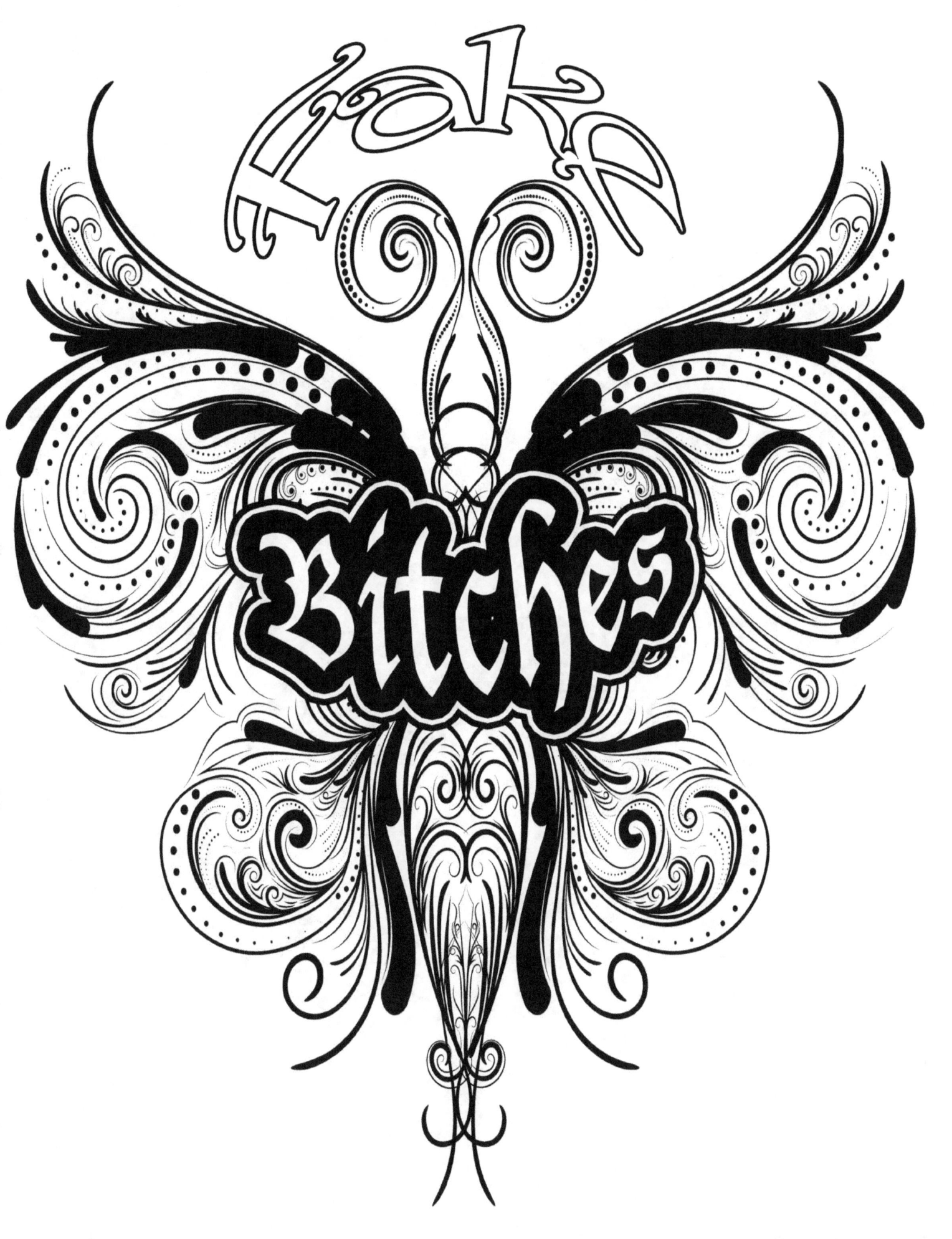

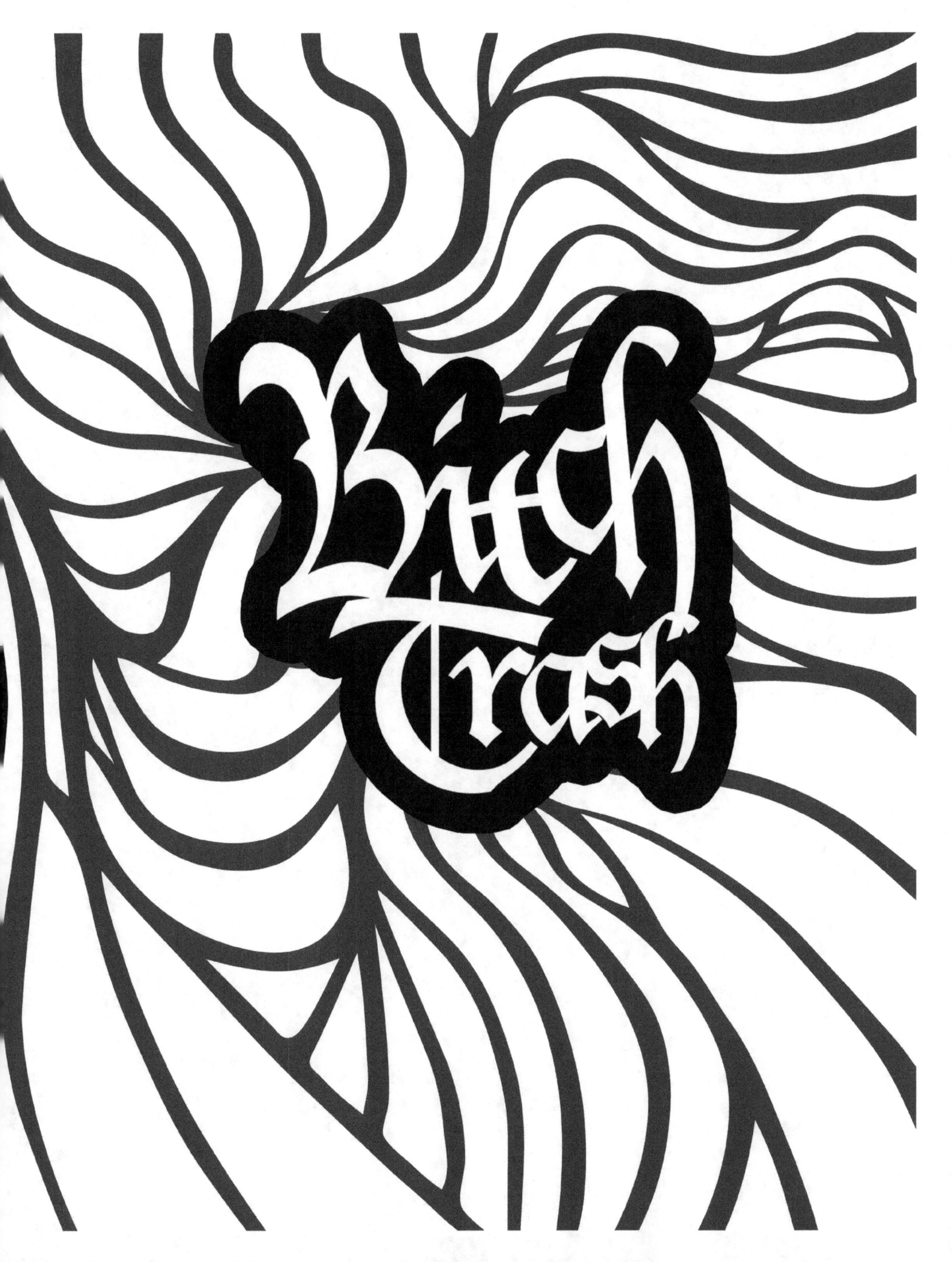

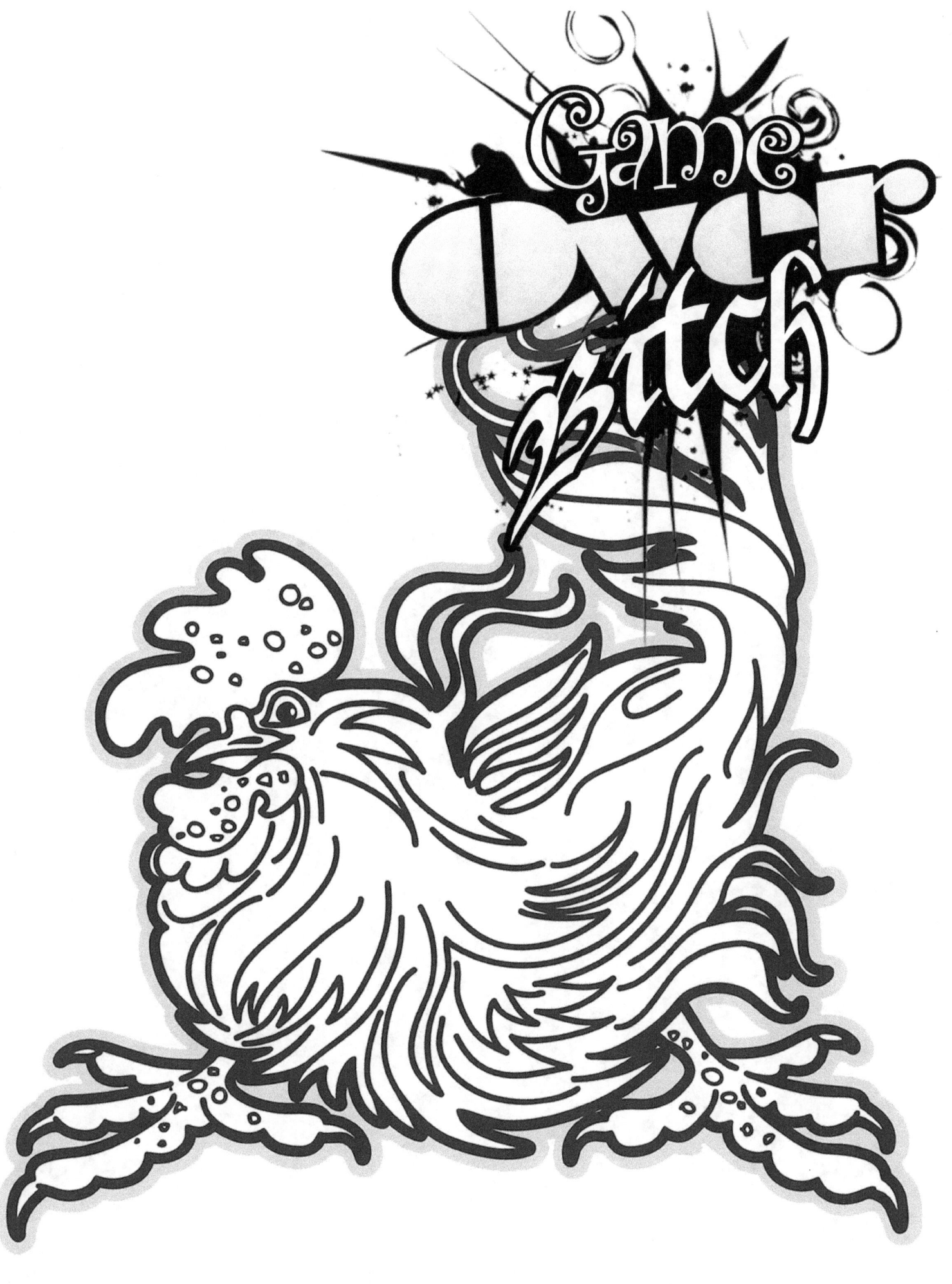

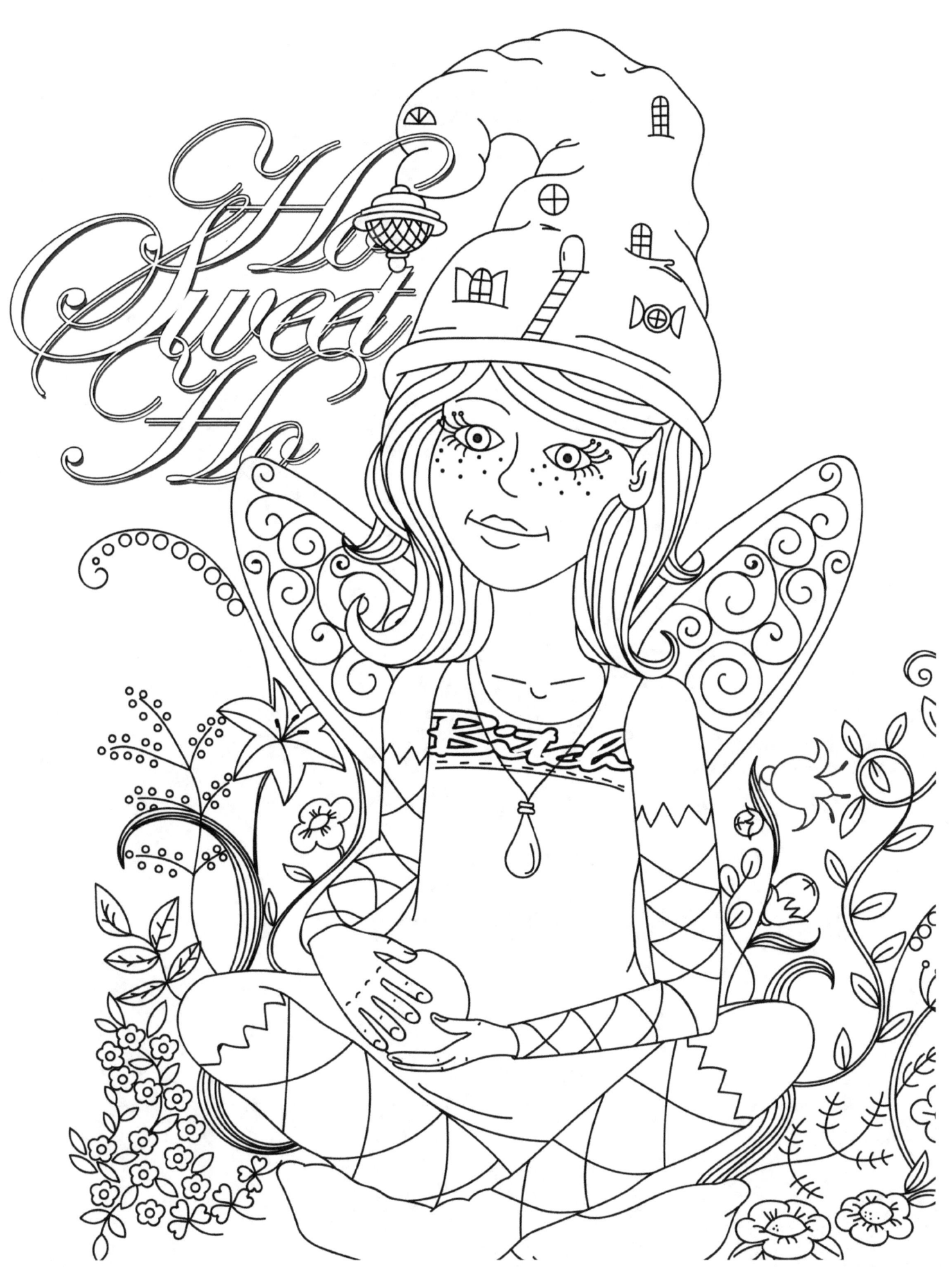

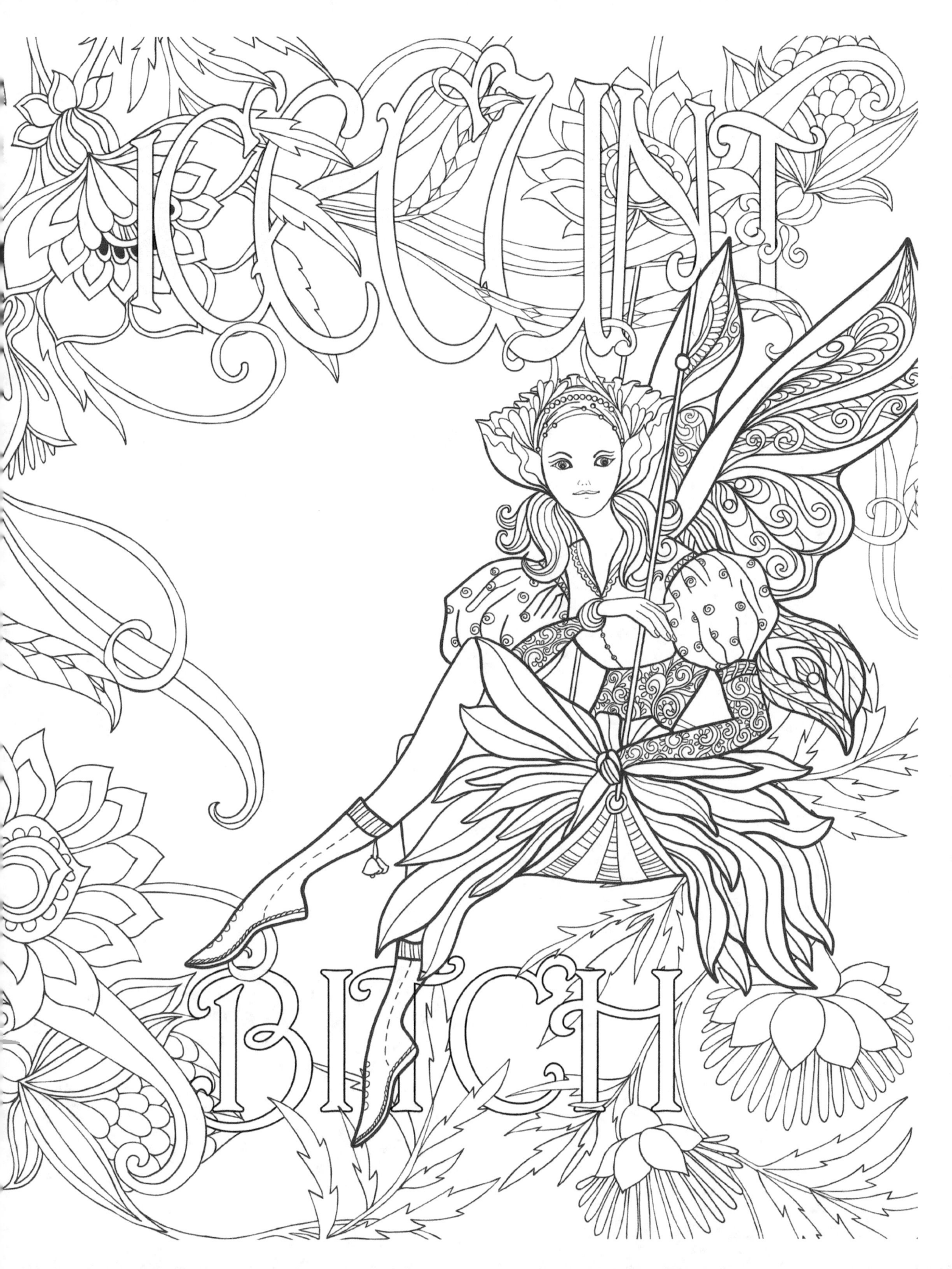

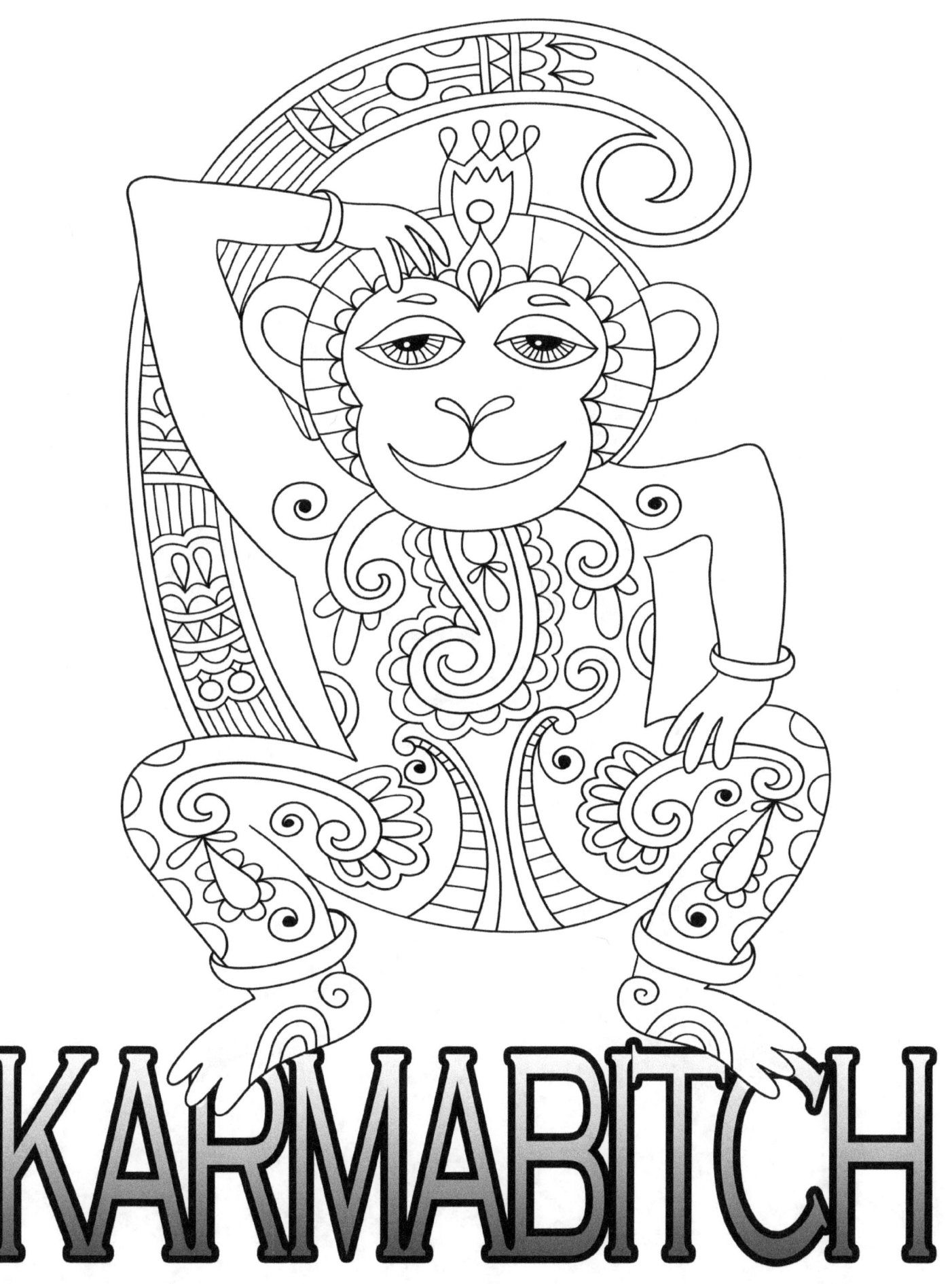

KARMABITCH

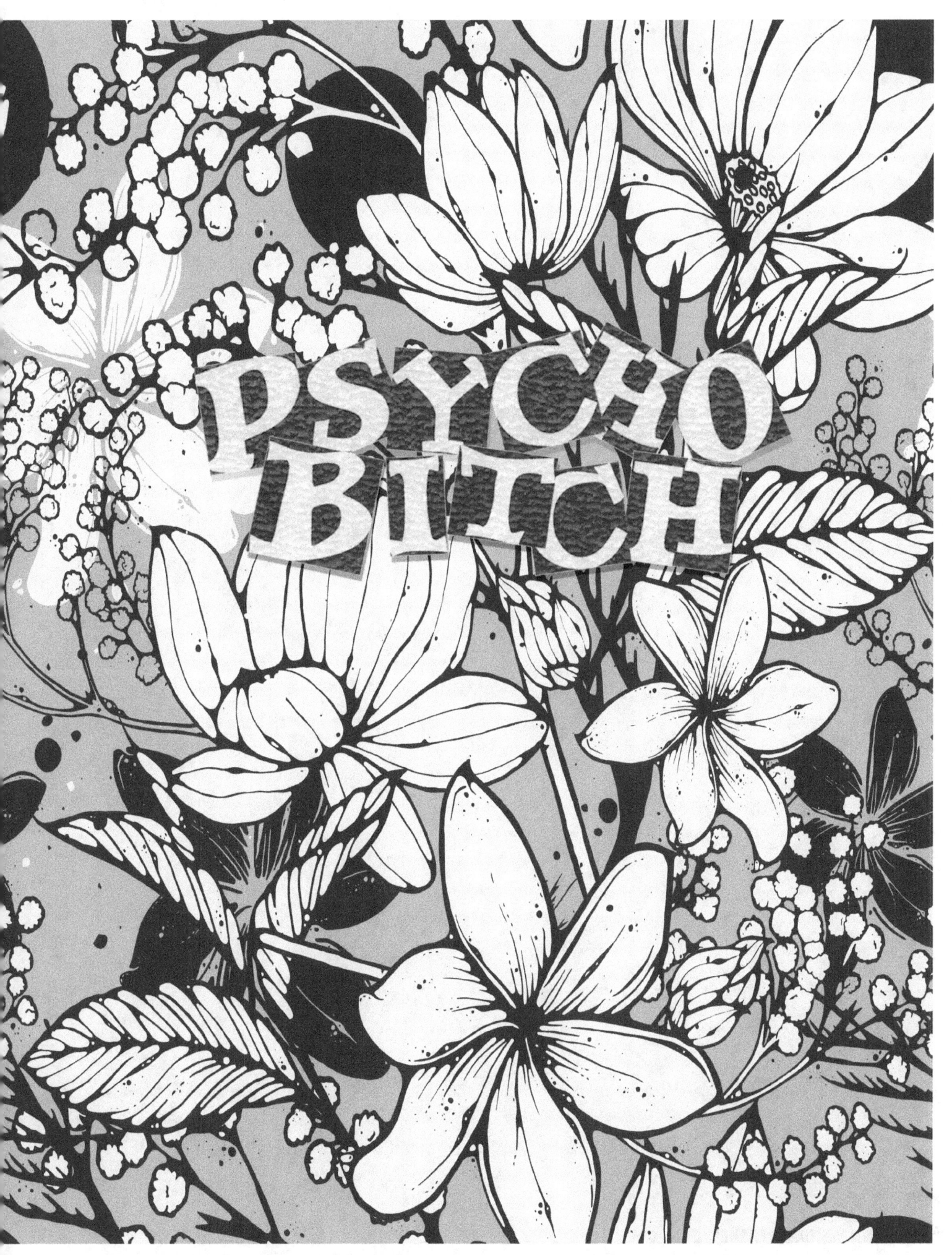